First Fabulous Facts

Scary Animals

591.65

Written by Anita Ganeri
Illustrated by Patrizia Donaera
Cartoon illustrations by Jane Porter

D0587263

004992971 2

Consultant: Dr Kim Dennis-Bryan

A catalogue record for this book is available from the British Library

Published by Ladybird Books Ltd
80 Strand, London, WC2R 0RL
A Penguin Company

001
© LADYBIRD BOOKS LTD MMXIV
LADYBIRD and the device of a Ladybird are trademarks of Ladybird Books Ltd

All rights reserved. No part of this publication may be reproduced,
stored in a retrieval system, or transmitted in any form or by any means,
electronic, mechanical, photocopying, recording or otherwise,
without the prior consent of the copyright owner.

ISBN: 978-0-72328-854-1

Printed in China

Contents

Which animals are scary?

Some animals have to be scary. They might need to fight off predators, catch food or protect their young. Some have sharp teeth and claws. Others have venomous fangs and deadly bites.

leopard

snake

crocodile

scorpion

Fabulous Facts

Deadly sharp

Lions are armed
with super-sharp
teeth and claws.
They use their
claws to catch
the prey and
hold it, while
biting it with
their teeth.

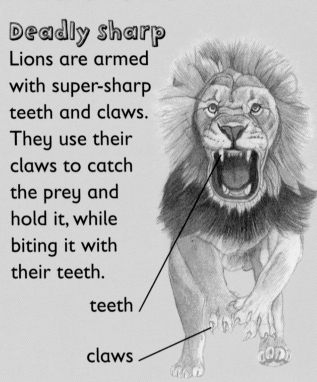

teeth

claws

Foul fangs

Some spiders have fangs in their
mouths, which they use to bite their
prey and inject venom into it.

wolf spider

Tiny terrors

The bite of the Anopheles
mosquito spreads a disease
called malaria. It kills about
600,000 people each year.

Wow!

Elephants are at least three times taller
than you are! Most animals leave them
alone because they are so huge.

Hello up
there!

Scary bears

Bears have big, powerful bodies, sharp teeth and long claws. They use these to catch their food. Female bears will fiercely fight off other animals, including larger male bears who try to attack their cubs.

adult bear

bear cub

Fabulous Facts

Big and biggest

Polar bears live in the freezing Arctic north. They are the biggest type of bear. Standing at about 2 metres high on all fours, polar bears are taller than an adult human.

Up here!

American black bears love honey. They use their hook-like claws to climb trees and reach it.

Mmm... honey!

I seal you

Polar bears hunt for seals by waiting next to holes in the ice. When a seal comes up for air, the bear catches it with its paw.

Hurry up, I'm hungry!

Wow!

Brown bears in coastal parts of North America are experts at salmon fishing, catching up to forty fish a day! They stand in the river and grab the salmon with their long claws.

That was mine!

7

Big cats

Lions, leopards and other big cats are strong and speedy hunters. They chase or follow an animal, then pounce suddenly. Their teeth and claws are used as sharp, deadly weapons to catch and kill their prey.

snow leopard

Himalayan tahr

Fabulous Facts

Clever camouflage

A tiger's stripes make it hard to see in the long jungle grass as it creeps after its prey.

You can't see me!

Tree lunch

A leopard eats its prey up high in a tree, far away from hungry lions and hyenas, who will try to take its food.

Time for lunch!

Team hunters

Female lions hunt their prey in teams. One lioness chases after a zebra, then another pulls it to the ground.

Wow!

Tigers do not usually eat people, but in the early 1900s, a fierce tiger in Nepal, Asia, reportedly killed and ate more than 400 people in just eight years!

Yikes!

Crunching crocs and alligators

Crocodiles and alligators mostly eat fish and turtles, but big crocodiles are powerful enough to catch large animals, like wildebeest. They swim slowly towards their prey, catch it and drag it underwater to drown.

wildebeest

crocodile

Fabulous Facts

Roll of death

When a crocodile pulls its prey underwater it rolls over and over to pull it to pieces. This is called a 'death roll'.

Crocodile or alligator?

You can spot the difference between a crocodile and an alligator by looking at their teeth when their mouths are closed.

You can see a crocodile's top and bottom teeth.

You can only see an alligator's top teeth.

Wow!

Mother crocodiles sometimes look as if they are eating their young. But they only put them in their mouths to carry them to water.

Look, no hands!

Gently does it!

Deadly sharks

Some sharks are fearsome hunters, especially the great white shark. Its huge mouth is lined with rows of about 3,000 jagged-edged, sharp teeth. If it loses a tooth, it is quickly replaced by another one!

great white shark

Fabulous Facts

Speedy shapes

Many sharks have pointed snouts, triangular fins and sleek bodies. This helps them to speed through the water at up to 95 kilometres an hour, almost as fast as a car on a motorway.

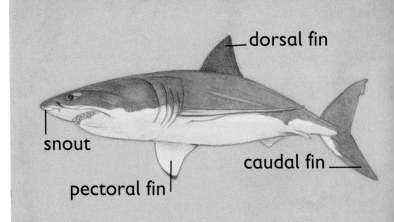

Super smell

A shark can sense the blood of an injured animal in the water from 500 metres away. That is about ten lengths of a full-sized swimming pool.

Smells yummy!

Deadly shake

A shark often grabs its prey in its jaws, then shakes its head from side to side to break off chunks of flesh.

Grrr!

Wow!

In 2012 a surfer in California, in the USA, was lucky to survive a shark attack. He fought off the shark by punching it on the nose!

Take that!

13

Scary sea creatures

There are lots of scary creatures in the sea with stinging spikes, spines or tentacles. The box jellyfish, which is found in the Pacific Ocean, has a sting that can kill a person in less than three minutes.

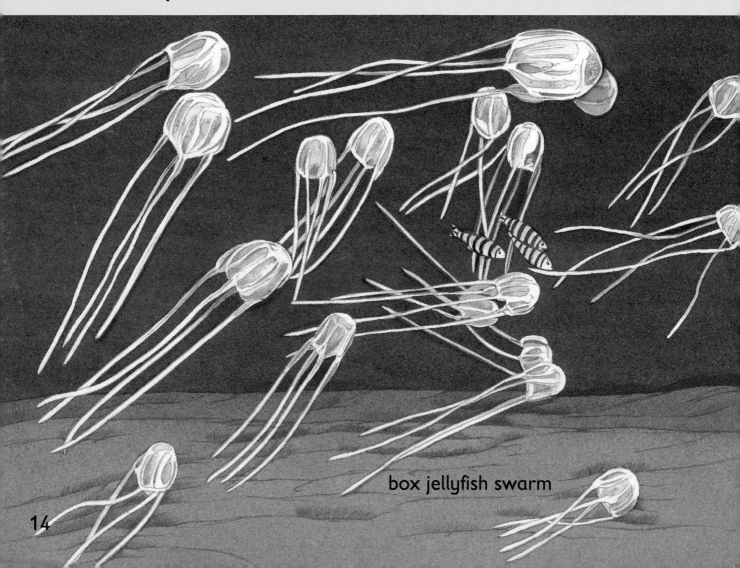

box jellyfish swarm

14

Fabulous Facts

Blue danger

A blue-ringed octopus is usually shy and hides away in holes in the rocks. But if something disturbs it, its blue rings glow brightly and it can give a deadly, venomous bite.

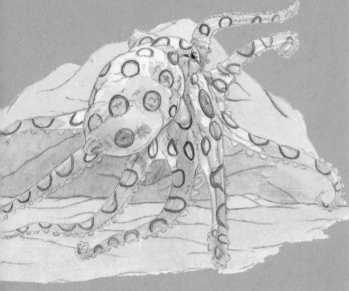

Stony stinger

A stonefish looks just like a stone, sitting on the seabed. But it has sharp spines on its back fins. These squirt out deadly venom if the fish is attacked.

Killer cone

The beautiful cone snail can be deadly. It uses a tooth-like spear, called a radula, to catch and poison its prey.

Wow!

In Australia, some swimmers wear special 'stinger suits' when they go in the sea. These help to stop them getting stung by box jellyfish.

I look silly!

It's worth it!

Shady snakes

Snakes are reptiles that eat other animals. Some, such as vipers, inject venom into their prey with their sharp fangs. Others, like the boa constrictor, wrap their bodies round their victim and squeeze it to death.

prey

boa constrictor

viper

Fabulous Facts

Rattle battle

A rattlesnake has a scaly rattle at the end of its tail. It shakes this to warn off its enemies. If this does not work, the snake will strike.

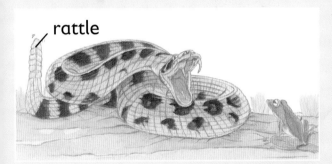

rattle

Nasty spit

The spitting cobra scares away enemies by spitting poison at them from up to 2 metres away. If it hits its attacker in the eye, the poison can blind them.

Fierce fangs

A Gaboon viper's fangs are up to 5 centimetres long. That's about as long as an adult's little finger!

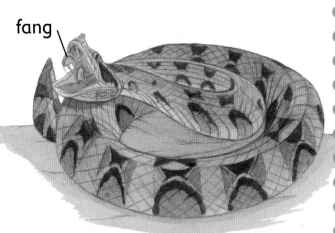

fang

Wow!

Snakes cannot chew their food. Instead, they open their mouths very wide, so that they can swallow their prey whole!

Yuck!

Gulp!

Sneaky spiders

Some spiders spin sticky webs to catch their food. Most spiders sink their fangs into their prey and kill it with venom. Big spiders, such as tarantulas, will hunt and catch mice, birds, frogs and lizards.

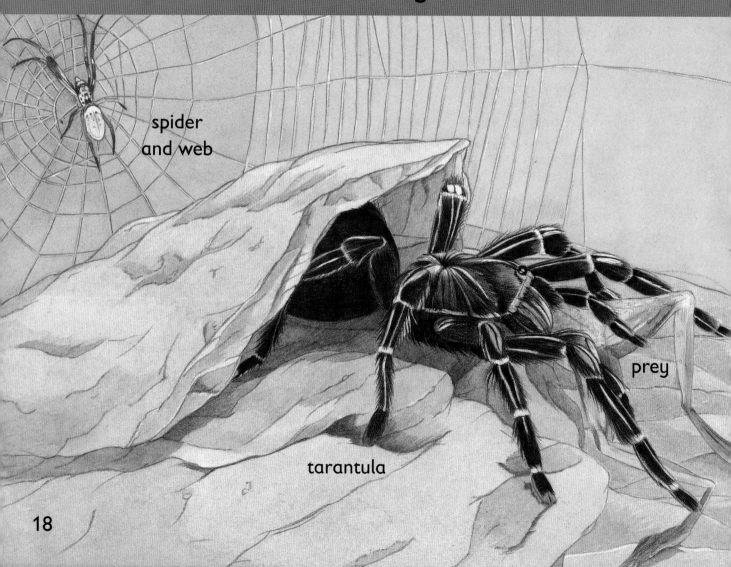

spider and web

tarantula

prey

Fabulous Facts

Don't sit down!

In Australia, deadly black widow spiders sometimes creep inside people's houses and spin their webs across toilet seats.

Big mouth

The spitting spider fires a poisonous, sticky liquid that it uses to trap and kill its prey all in one go.

Funnel webs

Funnel web spiders dig a burrow, then spin a funnel-shaped web over it. If an insect walks across the web, it shakes and the spider rushes out to kill it.

Wow!

The Goliath bird-eating spider is the biggest spider in the world. At about 30 centimetres across, it would fill your dinner plate. Yum!

19

Sharp stingers

With their black and yellow stripes, wasps and bees are easy to spot. But their bright colours are not simply for show. They warn hungry birds and other animals to leave them alone.

swarm of bees

Fabulous Facts

Busy bumblebees

Bumblebees are gentle insects with round bodies and soft hair. They only sting when threatened, but can do so several times.

Wicked wasps

Wasps are longer and thinner than bees. They are predators that sting and eat other insects.

Honey makers

Honeybees are smaller than bumblebees. When they sting, the stinger breaks off and the bee dies.

Huge hornets

Hornets are related to wasps, but can be up to three times bigger.

Good bees!

Bees are important because they help to make 70 per cent of the world's food crops. They do this by carrying the pollen that plants need to make seeds.

I love bees!

I love honey!

Wow!

The Asian giant hornet is the largest hornet. At 5 centimetres long, it is about the size of an adult's little finger. Its venom is very powerful and it can kill bees!

Buzz off!

Prickles and spines

Some animals have sharp spines and prickles for scaring their enemies away. A porcupine is covered in prickles called quills. If the porcupine is alarmed, it raises its quills to make itself look big and scary.

quill

porcupine

Fabulous Facts

Prickly puffer

The porcupinefish is covered in sharp, prickly spines. It puffs itself up to twice its size by filling up with water. This helps scare off predators.

Devil spikes

The thorny devil is a lizard from Australia. Its spiky body makes it look scary but it only eats ants! It can eat up to forty-five ants in a minute.

Spiky urchins

Some sea urchins have long, poisonous spines that they use to defend themselves and move across the seabed.

Wow!

The spike on a stingray's tail is like a very sharp, deadly venomous knitting needle. Ouch!

HELP!

Big and beastly

The size of an animal, like a hippopotamus or an elephant can be enough to keep attackers away. A hippo can weigh as much as two cars, while an elephant towers above most other animals.

hippopotamuses

Fabulous Facts

Deadly hippo

Hippos are one of the
deadliest animals in Africa.
Male hippos use their
huge teeth to fight. They
can cause terrible wounds
and even kill each other.

Noisy warning

Elephants guard their young
very fiercely. If an animal,
such as a lion, comes too
close, the elephant trumpets
and spreads out its ears. If this
does not scare the animal off,
the elephant will charge.

Wow!

If one African Cape buffalo in a herd
is attacked, all the others will run to
its rescue. Any animals in the way of
the stampede will be crushed!

Watch
out!

25

Night frights

Some animals seem scary because they are nocturnal. This means they are most active at night. Animals such as wolves, owls and bats hunt at night, dawn or dusk because there is more prey for them to catch.

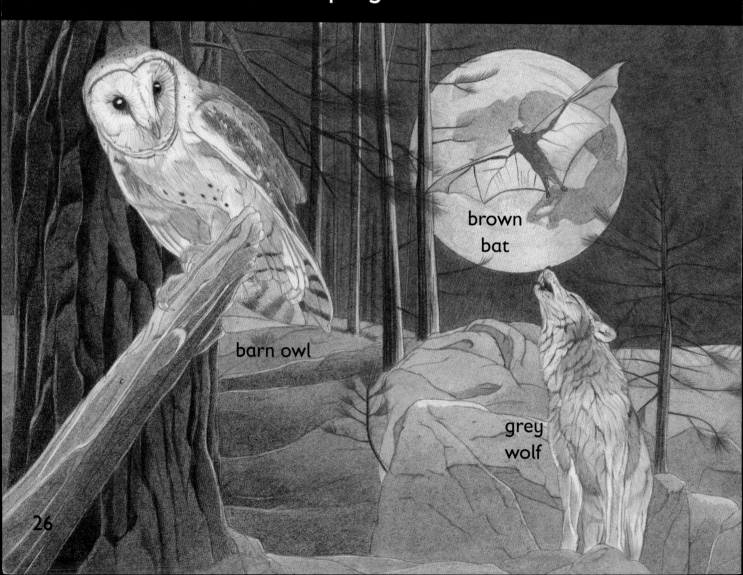

brown bat

barn owl

grey wolf

Fabulous Facts

Little devil

Tasmanian devils live only in
Tasmania, Australia. Their whiskers
help them hunt at night.
They have sharp
teeth and a very
powerful bite.

Daytime snooze

During the day, vampire bats sleep
in pitch-black caves or hollow trees.
At night, they head off to hunt.

They're hanging out!

Leaping lynx

The lynx is a large cat that hunts
alone at night. It creeps up on its
prey before quickly leaping out
to take it by surprise.

Yuck!

The vampire bat crawls on to an
animal's back and sinks its sharp teeth
in to make a small cut. Then it uses its
tongue to lap up the victim's blood!

I'm full!

Is there any more?

Record breakers

Deadliest snake

The fierce snake lives up to its name! Just one drop of its deadly venom is enough to kill one hundred adults!

Ancient monster

Megalodon was an enormous shark that lived over two million years ago. At 18 metres, it was three times longer than the largest great white shark that lives today. That's almost as long as two buses!

Most venomous frog

The golden poison dart frog is only 2.5 centimetres long (about the size of your big toe), but it has enough venom to kill ten adults!

Deadliest scorpion

If you live in north Africa, you need to look out for the Tunisian fat-tailed scorpion. The venom from its bite can kill an adult in just four minutes.

Strongest bite

The saltwater crocodile has the most powerful animal bite ever recorded. It is twenty-five times stronger than a human bite!

CRUNCH!

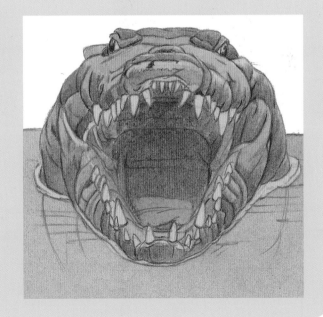

Beastly laughs!

Why do lions eat raw meat?

Because they can't cook!

What is stripy and bounces?

A tiger on a trampoline!

Where did the spider get married?

At the webbing!

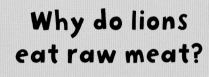

Why did the spider buy a car?

To take it for a spin!

What is an elephant's favourite drink?

Squash!

Which card game do crocodiles like to play?

Snap!

Glossary

fang   The mouth part or tooth of some animals that they use to hold prey and inject venom into it.

fin   The part of a fish or other sea creature that helps it move through water.

malaria   A deadly disease that is spread by mosquito bites.

pollen   A fine powder made by plants, which makes new plants grow when it is carried from one plant to another.

predator   An animal that hunts another animal for food.

prey   An animal that is hunted by other animals for food.

reptile   A cold-blooded animal that lays eggs.

spine   A hard, pointed part of an animal used for defence.

stampede   The sudden movement of a large group of animals.

tentacle   A long, bendy part of an animal that is used to hold things, or to move about. Some tentacles can sting.

venom   A fluid that some animals inject into other animals to poison and kill them.

venomous   An animal that uses a poisonous substance to attack other animals. For example, the blue-ringed octopus is a venomous animal.

Index